no fish

selected poems by

chris hall

published by

C*the*llective

Published 2019 by the Collective Press

Cover Design – Aneirin Jones based on original artwork by the author

Image of the author on publications page from a photograph by David Hall

Cataloguing in publication date for this book is available from the British Library

ISBN 978-1-913319-02-1

Published with no external financial support

Main Typeface: Gill Sans MT

Printed and bound in Great Britain by Empire Books

to my loved ones

Poems included in this publication were written and/or revised between 1971 and 20

Versions of the poems ilisted below have appeared in the following publications:

epigraf	*Quirk 5*
th wayfare v th white hare	*The Lonely Crowd 7*
five surrealist paintings	*Tears in the Fence 59*
a journey	*Scintilla 16*
a transylvanian tragedy	*Quirk 8*
aerthsong	*The Lonely Crowd 7*
th surgeon's sturgeon	*Quirk 8*
ornithografi	*Quirk 4*
no ifs	*Scintilla 22*
Dewi's Stone	*Tears in the Fence 59*
that year	*Quirk 10*
a neolithic tale	*Tears in the Fence 64*
nocturne at kindltide	*The Lonely Crowd 10*
on th final notes	*Quirk 10*

Versions of 'jonni-b', 'doggon skitsee 'and 'morph' were included in the chapbook/pamphlet 'Balladz f Bedlam' published by Stonebridge(2002), *and 'why i do not play cricket' appeared in 'Leg Avant' –* editor Richard Parker, Crater(2016)

Contents

epigraf

art is alkemi
it is   th taking v raw elements
    8   nd turning them into   fenomina

art is alkemi
it is not   mereli a depiction
            v visual landscapes
            or peopld streetseens
            nor th arrangement
                      v discoverd objects
            living
            still
            or otherwise

art is alkemi
it is   th taking v raw fenomina
            nd turning them into   earth

art is alkemi
it is not   cascading falls
            play v th waves
            th liquidising v pigment
            th trickl v tears
it is   th taking v raw elements
            nd turning them into   water

art is alkemi
it is not   th incandescents v th passions
            th leap n flicker v th striving imagination
            that flame that scorches
                      synapses nd ganglia
            volcanic eruptions
            notions v th incendiari
it is   th taking v fenominal elements
            nd turning them into   fire

art is alkemi
it is not   n act v pure transcendence
             above nd beyond
             th canopi nd panolpli
             a flight t th stars
             nor a fleeting glimpse
             v th face v th divine
             th cheating v death
             or a claim t immortaliti
it is
     alkemi   th taking v elementl fenomina
              nd turning them into   air

art is alkemi
it is not   quintysensuali relativ
             a matter v taste
             a means v defining
             reinvention
             scraps v
                   autobiografi
             psycho
                   therapi
             th charting v paradigms
             mapping v th mind
                       no more than
                  an assemblidj v signifiers
             t be imbued with
             postmodern ironi

             no no no

it is   empiricl
             extant
             everpresent

art is alkemi
it is   th taking v
             nd turning them into

th wayfare v th white hare

i have seen th white hare
                    scampa th night
                                        seeking th circl
                                        crossing th square
seen it caper nd scuttl
                    under th drift moon
                    neath briar n root
boxinclever
leaping th wikkid arc
spanning th awesome parabola

spied it hitherwards n thetherwards
                                        fording th brill
                                        blazing th purpl
reeling th ground over th heddihill
scudding between   apogee
                                                perigee
scaling th sky
            hurtling beyond fisick
                    beyond fantasm
                                        speculatid
                                        lusiv
                                        nonsubstantial
th woodland awaiting
                    nd i in attendance
                    sniffin th smoke
                    touching th mirrors
                    in that frail glade
            by th lost lair
            v th wan wild dove
                    furrowing innocence
                    feigning fertiliti
                                        at th rim v th lake
                                        neath th haunch v th hill

having not askt
since nor befor
ever whatnever
owt v those others
       others nd their seeing

th perceivance v th throng

nor anguisht whether
we had given
      harbour nd sanctuary
      t th ineffabl beast
          nd run th perimeter
          in th desolate day

f these things
matter but scarceli
      given th circumstance
      nd th perennial conundrum
         pondering th spaces
          twixt th words v cantankerous men

come th dawnbreak
in th raucous morning
      respite
      resurrection

  th aftercall   resonant in earshot

                    echolalia

n from th indefinite distance   th burnisht horn
                                                 a child's cry

daylong th wayfare
noonday th zenith   forshaddoing arrival
                                   th diurnal dilemma
                                   in th fluctuate light
                                   at th brink v cold summer
                                   portending autumn
                                   n th impendence v winter

nd at eventide
vespers
th traces v memori
recall
recapture

th quiet arrival
v th wicker guest

harbinj v
events recurring
          resolving   embers still burning

we th remaining

littl v it v our making

five surrealist paintings

th man standing

th man standing
by grey lake

by grey lake against crisp horizon
russitbrick wall;

in th foreground
crumblinartyfacts

grey lake
against horizon
russitbrick wall
nd in th foreground
plinth
sundial
caryatid

t th side
lampstand n shaddocast

bottom corner
red mullet

th woman
in her hand
hourglass

hourglass in her hand
at her feet
basilisk

over there
beyond basilisk
by th gramophone
orarari
lectern

beneath th lectern
early salmon

th young girl
beneath th linden;
by her side
hobbihorse
alongside hobbihorse   aardvark
                                    albatross

coalscuttl
candifloss

in th sky
two moons
gainst th skyline
glass mountain
waterfall

leaping th waterfall
dead centre
butterd turbot

infant boy
scampering towards
sunrise t th left
sunset t th right
crossing th canvas
deep dark forest
behind th forest   th deep dark forest
pyramid
eye   eye in th pyramid;

watching infant
th grayling

th cat
th black cat
staring from widowsill
out t th courtyard
n th empty phaeton
th scarlet fountain
th secret templ
th distant garden
th pathway t th pavilion
th rose in th orangery
purpl turtl
th writing on th carapace
th blood on th flagstone

no fish

a journey

beforehand
dissolving stars
sparkled on th surface
v th relentless
                    incoming tide

at dawn
she stirr'd
though none saw her rising
be it   from cradl nor carriageway
neither by pasture nor by portal
either behind th cedar
or beside th sea

in th morning
she laught
loud n long
nd those that were near her
in stabl or at staging post
marvell'd at her energy
her glee
th prancing step

mid-morning
she cried
though no-one dared venture
whether those tears
spilt beneath arbour nd canopy
flowing in th face
v mistral nd maelstrom
indicated grief or cathartic epiphani

at noon
she screamd
though those in earshot
standing by th breakwater
or riding th high tor
could not be sure
whether that shriek
was hollerd in ecstasi
abandonment
or in th sheerest v terrors

after th noontide
she spoke
yet no-one heard her
there on th promontri
in sight v th lighthouse opposite th cob
nd th clogs v th fishermen
nor did they notate
phrase or utterance
functional
            notional
                    or abstracted

at evening
there was silence
nd none could tell
be they passenger
            participant
or innocent bystanda
whether it signified
reflection at sunset
or th mute realisation
that nothing
            was as
                    it had ever
                            appeard t be

come nightfall
all that remaind
were the essentials

th knowledge that afterward
eternal stars
would sparkl from th depths
v an infinite universe
                        wherever nd forever
dark   here nd there
                    open t th possibilities
                        v a myriad illuminations

quintet

once he had sat
in th pretend café
listening t Satie
on th rudimentri headphones
just down
from th Roman baths

        (with their singular refurbishment
        v virtual water
                subfusc
                eerie lighting
      nd ersatz
             irrelevant music
      where famous poets
     on occasion
         read their work

  alongside creative writing students from th local college
  some v whom were studying history)

wondering precisely
how t word
th missive to
his friend th flautist
gently intimating
that his latest work
a putative quintet
         on a chamber scale
did not include
a part f her instrument
as he felt
its fundamentl sonoriti
was v a nature
all too human
n potentially sibilant
to express th essential spirituality
a central imperativ
v its basic aesthetic;

nd that he hoped
this present
creativ idiosyncrasy
would not impair
their longterm amiti
nor preclude
any further
          collaboration

it was
      with some distress
      she later learnt
                  that in his effects
                  they had found
                              sometime after
                              his gentl yet
                              inexplicabl death
a manuscript score
v an unfinisht opus
f th customari
                  four stringd instruments
                  along with

                  a tenor saxophone

initiall'd
not signd

as was his wont
as was his practice

truth lies

(written after an identification of Type 2 diabetes, the realisation that I had been in a state of denial for some time regarding my condition, and subsequent surmisings as to the act of lying to ourselves and others possibly being a default trait as far as human beings are concerned)

come summer
you will learn
why it is
you have been
albeit unknowingly
far too sweet
f yerrown damn good

that said
this we will find
hardly surprising
in light v th predictabl
benefits v hindsight
given th foregoing   (foregoing that is
                                                    in th meaning v precedence
                                                    rather than
                                                                    that which implies
                                                                    a sense v denial)

nd th perpetual recurrence
over th years
v degrees v imbalance
parallel with concealment
nd th inevitabl accompanying
question v appearances

spring having proven
beyond th luxurious illusion
a season v diagnosis
didactic prescription   fine red wine
                                            now t be
                                                            sipt not quaff'd
                                            th pleasurabl flesh
                                            there f th savouring
                                            rather than
                                            a subject v gluttony
                                            nd heroic excess

endemic extravagance
leading to
          th portals v delusion ;

nd behind those doors v deception:
                    mystification
                    obfuscation
th flights nd stairways
t disillusion
gnosis
revelation:

artistri being
take it or leave it
one step from artifice
a celebration v th illusory;
th domain v th spirit
bordering on
th realm v th sprite
                    piskie
                    brownie

call me Trismegistus
          waterfixa
          abbeylubber

call me boggart
          brag
          bucca
          dobie
          fetch
        ignis fatuus
    pinket
          perriwink

call me messenger
          magus
          merriman
        jackolantern
    maker v   rubedo

  th magnum opus

listen: listen nd hark
harken th silence
                sostenuto
nd with it
a spherical music   drifting across
                              ethers nd eons
from a place where once we stood
here by th grainy door
longside th chizzld window
opposite th performance place
where th singer sang
twixt th jaunt v th juggler
nd th scoff v th fireater
                              (or rather
                                      as it transpired
                                                      th blow)

that place where
excludid trombonists
nd included fiddlers
did what it took
n took what it was
nd confessional poets
exuded therapi nd expressd nothing
or at least
            it should be said
                                  very little
                                          beyond themselves

nd over there   th ebony pumps
                                      with th copper inlay
rest mute
behind that porcelain   pink with glaze
indecipherabl beneath its ornamentation
nd th downward glance
v th willowy muse
in th shallo pre-Raphaelite painting

yes indeed
here we stood
by this pond
on this mound
envelopt in th green mist
on th stranger's hill   high above th city lights
stippld by th droplets
briefly imagind sounds
from way out there on th heathland

          n someone said
          a long time after th event
          we were happy here
          or maybe not
                    not all th time anyway
                    not all v th time

nd yes yes
reflection recalls
melodi was made here
under th summer willow
here nd in th darker streets
with their scent v heaven nd th hints v hades
n in th coverd market
cavorted here
made merry here
high heaven n merry hell here

here where th dusk rose n th morningtide fell
across th shimmer v night nd th shaddo v th day

nd here we danced   dallied n danced
at th earth's arising
n th world's end   yes made merry
                              merry mayhem
                           music n mayhem here
                         thriving nd writhing here
                              writhing n thriving

seizing th clout
casting th moment
grasping th mettl here

n let it be said
            said here
that there it is
here where it was
there where it is
                there nd here
                here n there

hither
thither   whether
                                        wherever

given time
upon th discerning
this being summer
you will discover
like th budded iris
th perfumes v   delian paradisials
                        nd sultry coltranes
shimmering upon
th evening air
harbingers v   faeri nights
                        nd elvan days   assumptions
                                                 maskerades

then   come midnight
                              an unpredicted unveiling:
                              unveiling nd unravelling
th removal
v delightful pretence   nay
                                    bray
                                        delving down
at a last resort   down deep
getting to
th bottom v th thing

nd on th landing
you will hear   whispers
                                      whipperwills

these secrecies:

nd with them
th concomitant untruths   (that is
                                        lies not falsehoods)
there being
a certain veracity
inherent in
th fantom gateways
nd acts v huggamugga
          camouflage
culminating
in th disclosure
that after some   deliberation
th truth lies   in th contradictions

sensing
after all th echoes nd th resonances

it is th living v it
     th living   living v it

wetland

osmosis

th membrane

netherplace

(nether naether
ether aether)

        chime

        peal

        garner

a resoundant tolling

tide

tide nd time

let me be
let me be there

sated

no longer emergent

mystified

explosiv

and th tale
nd th teller   flying

                                                  wingless

                                      random

                                                  guilty

                                              lost

                                                  tumbling

                                          redeemd

over sea
over canopy

    tundra

                th sanstone shaddos
                nd in th wetland depths

riding th rime

wading th wayward waters

fathoming sublimiti

a transylvanian tragedy

in parenthesis
th garlic lookt
hardly amiss
hanging there
uneaten

in parenthesis
th angl at which
th bat clung
provoked no argument

in parenthesis
th elegant traveller
evinced no comment
excepting that
concernd with th sartorial

n yet
he thought
wincing in reflection
something untoward was amiss

it wasn't that
discretion botherd him
nay even
th tilt v th tumbler
emitted nothing
but fresh red wine

yet still it came t pass
as he sat
idle v aspect
in conspiracy with th saxophomist
wishing t burn mountains
wondering which ace t play
th stupid remembrances
v all those lies nd lays
pushd th sombre
t th back v his mind
as night   crept on in

at length
th countess n th count
suckt him dry
as they had done
his total ancestry   and
      in that strange morningtide
      he would inherit
         dirt n pinewood
th strains v jazzmusic
      emblaznd upon th dawn

there they found him
th jester n th mastermind
nd there they built him
only a tiny monument

n as y pass by
in th wake v y journeyings
you will find
that y put away
y quill n journal   leaving rebirth t history
      nd his dark deeds
      t th cartografa

aerthsong

these littl rivulets
sparlklindownstream
bearing with them
spawn n sticklback
by now
                coming t confluence
by now
                bringing broom
                bringing brushbundl
                burbl n larchenleef

n with th current
                                separation
                                rejection

                                                disjunction

                                                trauma

                                                alienation

nd by now
on th bankside
Anselm th Shepherd
whistlz his dogs
up from th sheep-pen
glancing dolefully
with fear n trepidation
at th hired hand
approaching him through th turnstile
with tidings from th dippingplace

by now   after th sunlight
Magdelena
will leap from her bed
determind t put aside
her tendency t shatta hearts
resolving with some degree v certainty
t bake th most
                    splendid v bread
t distribute around th neighbourhood

by now
th city will have opend its gates
nd th grand caravan
v minstrels nd haberdashers
paraded beyond th marketplace

nd under th chiming clock
Pavel th Moravian
will be revealing all kinds v mysteries
t th children v th silversmiths
n th denizens v th outhouses

by now
tides will be turning on th furthest v shores
nd th Daft Old Bastard n th Blithering Idiot
will be commencing their discourse
on th Nature v Beatitudes nd th Rationales v Retribution
as is usual
devoid v n audience

while over at th bonded gallery
people with strange ears nd stranger eyes
will have pontificated just enough
t make sense
v th most explanatori nd least contentious v images

nd across town
there in th printshop
Berenice th journeywoman
pushes th dedline n hammers th furniture

producing
                under cover v daylight
her limitid editions
v borderline conspiracies
nd esoteric scriptures
bound in vellum nd in venom
packt
posted
deliverd
                t th furthest v libraries
                n th darkest v depositories

nd th Blithering idiot will tug at th garment
v th Daft Old Bastard nd exclaim loudly
"there: there; wasn't I telling ya
didn't I go betcha"

n th Daft Old Bastard will hack at th tabletop
nd growl *sotto voce*
"whispa goddammit: whispa y idiot;
y Blithering Idiot…"

n by now
th season will speak
nd th time will tell
n we v all people
will have opend our hearts
t th most magical v choruses
nd our severd souls
t those magnificent descants   high
                                high
                                        in th sky
                                            gannit glide
                                            nd lapwing fly

                                        lark hover
                                        eagl swoop
                                        swift n swallow
                                        loop th loop

yes by now
Kingdom Henry n Marjorie Mankerthank
might have found consolation
after all those
years v heartache
                        their travels t th hinterland
                        th evenings in th cellar bar
but
    it would appear
                        inexplicably
                        not with each other

f by now
th good doctor
n th nastinurse
will have considerd th pharmaceuticls
that will provide a prognosis
v barely perceptible recovery
f their most
                        recalcitrant v patients

nd though their efficaci
could never be questiond
they may well
postpone their ministrations
n substitute their toxins
f various placebos

                n over by th tapestri
                th tenor saxophonist
                nd th tone-deaf trombonist
                will agree t finally
                settl their differences
                by burying th hatchet
                squarely in th horn
                v th dentally afflictid cornettist

"so what
by now?"
says th Daft Old Bastard
"what what:
by now"
says th Blithering Idiot
grabbing hold v
nothing really   nothing v any substance

 yes...yes by now
it will be gatherd
th crisis v identiti
has nothing t do
with th pinnacl v mania
or th depths v depression
nor there again
th vagaries v DeoxyriboNucleic Acid

rather be it
th bald truth
you have no knowledge
nd caught no sight
v who it was
who might have preceded you
given shape
          feature
          tone
          n temperament

nd that
after all these years
it is
time t let   let n let leave
bygones be bygones
nd put aside th lookinglass   slow th climb
                                      swift th fall
                                 hard th th tumbl from th wall
                                 t th place where waters flow
                                    n HumptiDumpti says hello

but then
y should anyway
by now
have reached that spot
in sight v mudflats
where y once espied kingfishers
n trampt across scrubland
in search v pheonices
transmogrifications
           hulks
           habitats   real revolutions

again then nd   then again
here where th river curls
n th tall trees
shelter their secrets
you have found
some kind v quietude
under th canopi

n those altars magickly constructed
                        be they from remnants
                        v th Holiest v Holies
                        or from those twilight places
                        v Pagan Profaniti
linger there still
in th forgotten glades

nd there within
th capricious alcove
th Daft Old Bastard holds up his hand
t shield his tired eyes
from yet one more revelation
whilst th Blithering Idiot
oblivious t machinations n t miracles
shakes a dismantld fist
at all th bygones nd th by whens
th by thens nd th by nows   th was nd th is
                                      th once were n th will be

n you wander n wonder
whether it is
by now
Arriaga th Anarchist
could have begun t realise
after his debates
with factionl elements
n others who ought t have known better
that th collaps
        v th Soviet Union
           would never result in
      somekindv
          libertarian utopia
     nor even
     th re-establishment v first principles

nd you can glimpse
Dorothea from th faculti
turn t her friend
           as she travels onwards
           on a stopping train
           up towards th tundra

nd surmise
    who wouldv thought it all them years ago
    that by now
        th primary resistence
        t th global pandemic
        v transnational capitalism
        would seem not t come
        from th triumph v th progressively modern
        but emanate out v
        resurgent mediaeval
        notions n nostrums

nd her companion considers
n gently responds
that this might well be
an inevitabl reaction
against th sad fact
that all th ingenuiti nd invention v th Enlightenment
have by now
culminated in
various acts
v human degradation
being avidli viewd
on th plasma lantern
by both lumpen n learnid
as a signal manifestation
                    v mass entertainment
amid th racket
v ubiquitous cacophoni

                              wait on here
                              f i have grown older
                              wait on here
                              f i have got colder

                              hang on in
                              times have grown tougher
                              hang on in
                              th world has got rougher

n so
by now
all that remains
is th faintest v false hope
that those
          long ago
                    tiny streams
are by now
an unstoppabl torrent
straining behind
th walls v th dam

nd that
when th concrete nd th brickwork burst
th floodtides will bear with them

                along with th debris
                nd what remains
                v a millenium v architecture

th supreme surges
v life nd love
life in th sinews nd love in th arteries

            love behind th volumes
          that fester on th bookcase

            love beyond th musicstand
         in th corner v th cabaret

      love on th waterfront nd love in th crazi cloister
      love on th ice nd love in th fire

           love in th departure
         th journey nd th arrivl

           love in th complexity v th calculus
        nd in th simplest v equations

      in hours v pertinence nd moments v distraction
      in th totally unrehearst
nd in that which overwhelms utterly

          nd in all that conveys
               nothing nd everything

             ever nd forever

          in th silence n th ceasing

             never nd f never

from all those   consummate endings
n what is left v   unconsummated beginnings

there will be   love t th east

                                    love t th west

                                  love t th south

                             n love in th north
nd this be so
because by now
i have learnt
        th lyrics v th aerthsong

an can say
    can say with some finaliti
this time
without fear v contra
           diction
things are
when it comes t th essentials   good

                     good

                        good

                      good

                    good
                     bye now

fenician

times when
messiahs raged
nd cut their kindred
he kept counsel

occasions that
choirboys n spindthrifts
laid them end t end
silence was his byword

thus it was
around fall
when warlocks avenjd him
n blind faith
         never th keenest v diadems
left its mark on th walls v th workhouse
he chose
         t stake his claim upon millennium
         somewhere at th back end v th sun

in th beginning
th glare dazzld him
cauterizing th worthless partition v reason
unbelittld
nd t th observant lens
th traces v blood
fleckt by th sharp edge v th eggshell
across th surface v his intial skin
offendid
         only th most literate

he survyvd
though jokes n sinecures
were never t his liking   yes
he survyvd   without wraps
                                without baublz
nd in his wanderings
he would have chosen
never t die
one v these   experimentl deaths:

v a sudden   made narrative
v a sudden   vivid
                                unearthd
a veiny being in a negated age
spirit scorcht n painful upon th breath
came he t places
                preternatural

nd there
in th parchd heat v th hurricane
huskt n ashen v eye
th spectre claimd him

thus celebrant
thus mandrake
sacramental nd abrim with sap
drew he at length
t where they coincide   th cradl n th furnace

nd as with antichrists n frail dancers
th flame itself
put an end t him:

in these days   debauchd by pity
                          astonisht at mercy
in these days
taken by forces   less than molecular

you nd i
recoil   look each other
                         up n down

                         waging th war on behalf v bastardy
                                  eager t waylay
                                  decisive tidings
                                  concerning th fate v th yule

yet
even at this strange hour
when they choke th living daylights
nd ask if it   were all foretold
i still stare out at
those unquencht essences
those
        forester's tales   and

th surgeon's sturgeon

th sunderer
       born v contempt
took hold v th fishknife
nd set it
with a certain exquisite perception
t th rear v th gills:

th scream
emanating from that
       global liquid eye
held no surprises
f one who accepted
th open-mouthd
       acts v respiration
         peculiar t fishes

n with his scalpel   (lately wielded
       f th benefit v
         sullied livers
         brief intestines;
       then
       patiently returned t th sheath
       ready
         without th luxury v greed
       f th summons t dissect
       th next delicaci)

incised th contours v his skull with virtuosity
n placed his brain
ungarnisht upon th altar

th fish
equipt with th vision   v merely two sides
blinkd n
n flapt its fins   at th dryness
       v so much

       fresh air

doggon skitsee

littl bitter sparkl: Twinklin-I!
littl sharp spectacuLAH: Sir Prize!
hergest harden howlin Houndv Hell!
a-whalen atme Fragmenten Disguise:

inme Vaughstate, upper pon th ridj
th canine cri qui-quikkenin inme breast
me-Dreamcom! nd th dark distinctif Whine
YOWLS t dewpond, wherri lies at rest.

downin hamlets, on th Borderline
th LIAR nd th LAFFINstock n Priest
cohort tgether cross th oaken floor
t bring me fetterd t th Hallowed Feast;

nd there upon th Tabl they will set
th Lovincup, th Lixir v me youth:
nd from me SHATTERD SOUL bi Three Degrees
extract from me th essents v me Truth.

from thence t Funnifarn thell bear me up
wi Thump o Tabor, nd with CLANG v Bell;
nd thus will smiler Soothe nd Scythe nd Steal:
n pricken sesame will make me Well.

yet Here-Within-th-Dark will I remain;
immune t Faith, t Flippantfate, or Fear:
nd hurtlincross th starface nd Vast Voids
th Dewpond Voice will speak...AND I WILL HEAR!

ornithografi

out there
what cacofoni
what sheerbrill songfest
     wingy tweetwarbl
          n beaken concertante
          carillon v chirp nd chirrupchant
n th whole sprung symphony
v birdborne avianity
crest n call
trill n wren nd rusti robin

here within
snug n smug nd fireside warming
     sublime artifice
        resounding round th room
        Bruno Walter's brimming Beethoven
            Pastoral symphony number six
            movement two

            brookscene
            waterflow nd lapping stream
            flutingale
            oboe quail
            cuckoo clarinet

yardwise
open air beyond th pane
featherflutter flight aflap against th winter chill
ravenous n raucous
frantic in th line v sight   finch
                   titmouse
                   redbreast

            on th eyeline
            within earshot
            fortissimo molto
th real thing

chantreuse

deemd animal
she came on in
        out v th forests
        out v th swampland
came in t cities
        uttering prehistory
       seeking fabulousnesses
           bred v a primitive science;

deemd animal
she came on in
        out v th sunlight
        sometime after:

n perhaps
th latterday curse
        betoknd in incident
        gatherd in th backrooms nd across landings
belied her masteri;

no matter said she
i have seen dead sons
creep out between th silences
n th wanton glories v my flesh
were not t be lost
on th signposts v my daughters
           left unsaid
           within th contours n cultures
v an intimidatid universe

th crippld bartender
watcht her performances
wildly
        through his glass eye   (revolutionary that he be)
        n polisht th keys v th upright
        t mystify her songs:

nd yet
f all this gaudy magick
the age
        lay still a-dying;

soldiers nd deridid queens
rememberd her epigrams
purely spasmodically;

all those heroes
taught her by warmongers n granpappas
rarely emitted
any kind v
            mystic flamboyance
nd dukes n old men
bargaind in th aisles n urinals v her craft:

singularly did she tug at th sun
t wrench it t th night-time;
singularly nd singl
did she parade th riverbank
looking f toads
n other amphibians;

at outside tables nd on inside stools
her chant could be pickt out   being spent;

deemd indeed
of nd amongst th poor
was she left t wander
th spires n stumbling blocks
now refuted
                as she crumbld in th alleyways

there so she be
beyond mythology
siezen by th medicinl
incarcerated by th contrasympathetic
when nemesis came a-calling
nd left there wailing
defeated by th substance
n confoundid by th illusion:

    come th coda
    a transpired awakening
      thru an unpredicted
           (nd in th main
              virtually unsought)
        series v revenges
    both extravagant nd inconspicuous
    nd certain familiar
           hitherto unexpected
                educings n rememberings

thus
at th instant v denial
          denying nothing
unafeard v th onslaught v spring
catching th voice n finding th lilt

casting aside
th parsifals n th morganas
nd dancing on th dream
          (bold th intoning
          th ear resonant)
              libertine her meanders
              unfetterd her return

with a nod t th croupier
turnd her arse t th all v it

and
        at th first dawn

cascadid
    smouldering
                    (torchin
                        scorchin)

    ubiquitous nd inescapabl

    onward t th perimeters

expansiv

shameless

                        hailing th hench v her

        definitiv
            valedictori

                ringing th riley

                claiming transcendence

jonni-b

these three fellahs, see;
these three damkwirchaps
meandr in Outer
outv th twilandlight
outta th SUNSCUTTL
bankinon tryin it:
(som would say triuphan -
som would say Fortunat)
cartin connivance
Solemnvow (massacr)
jonni b y'ungamman
Jon: yerra Dedman.....(JONNI-b: deddenman)

nd These Three See KWIRFELLAHS
these three three Rkityps
givvim th one-two thrice
givvim th Sunderin
leavvim t kittyhawk
leaf f th Raggltag..........Then

RAINCOMDOWN!

(unearth underearth
whatta Pallarva!
fallabaht LAFFINat
fallapart Festrin)

nd that jonni-B see
thatbugga Jonni B........he
pokes it out sneakilike
(solemnvow? NUN'V IT!)
ere y kin ketchim

uppuPPigrows..........Therri goes!
springstep b'Fuddlz y
maze:maize: AMAYZIN y
standthere till suppatime
STAND-RITE-THERE Midsummer
madness nd pallorwan
Close: no-shave; beardigro
(so? sow: th so-n-so)
sow:sew; nd so so so   AND SO BECAME A MAN

falltime - th Cuttascum
sheer: Scythen: brishinhook
kneebrichen cuttiscut
rangl, roll, wrappenwrack
pitchFork nd pykenstaff
Loda - n worstenat!
(servd Him most Barbrousli):
boundim t Cart...

(UPearth: manifest
giv me me Waterspout Jonni-b: Pleasant Chap
guzzl me Shuvldown
herein th Corridor
GIVE US A BREAK!)

Hoist up! th wheeliround
See how th   YOU'RE NO USE!
chukkimin Barn..........
o Poor Jonni B!
jon b; Be: barleycorn
cuttin wi crabtreestix
shakim fr'm Mainsailshaft
skinnim from Bone.
(nd that old Millerman)
that gristygrindyman
stoneSCREECHstone:turnaround
pulp: POWder: pummldown
                        down
                        t th Last

OH! Oh th Firmament !
(that's what th Ferment meant)
yeast: east: th torment ceasd
pourd in th Pewterjug
Lovli in Lushousness:
Thisbe th pentecost
Praise be t jonni B!
Here's to y, Good John B,
Issue v Barley corn!
Plenish th Glass!

(y could say
spied immin th alehouse

      nutbrown
      deepdown................LAFFINlast

havina giggl   at y'r expense)

no ifs

i am a man more
sinnin than cinder genst
having emerjd
out v th great no where
uttering onli
screechen catterwaul
              from th outset
                   dreaming alone
                       nd given t ructions
                             whyforwayfare
ever th tendenci
              t th magnetic poles

it was however
yonder by th lichgate
that th first hints v th heathen
gave way t th hymns v th heretic
nd those fierce visions
(yes i said visions)
v a prophesied
                 here nd now

nd when they said
it was
     time t wake up
shaking th cradl nd smashing th skylight
i held clenchtight
t th tenets v th dreamstate
nd th imperativs v nightmare

t this day
there cannot be
even th slightest
                    trace v regret
nor spurious soothsaying
                        no ands
                        no buts
amendments
codicils
        th one truth being
        beyond all others
                        there are no ifs in histori

this then was
                th starting point
                th setting out
shorn v manifesto nd v balderdash
unlaydnd nd unburdnd
by th encumbrences v ancestri
blind tradition
tyranni v
        a semblant inheritance

so when y ask me
how come
i sit here in th windoseat
cracking th heads from shellfish
n pretending t be
                part v th graffiti
th reply
tho not necessarily   elydid
                    purposefulli obscurantist
will still be
in need v   deconstruction
                        discernment

                some measure
                        v disentangling

nd maybe
(yes i said   just maybe)
i might have answerd
that they came looking
f a younger man
full v hope
        springsong
        a measure v empathi
        iskra
        that spark

nd yet
(yes yet)
it can still be promulgated
that in this dreamin city
those fine
(so fine)
butresses fly
against them surjinspires

nd i espy
down there by th riverbank
that old bridge
clings on regardless
                    v wagonloads
                        vagabonds
                            th muleteers

nd in th end
(if end there be)
let it be said
there was onli
one passage possibl
nd that would always be
th one that was taken

now
when night comes
i will myself surmise
was it here?
or there?
or someplace in th great wherever
that which was lost
can be now be retrievd
                gatherd
                comprehendid?
nd will
even i   sinbad th sinnaman
as a last resort

look up t th vast expanse v th highest v all th heavens
nd th lowest depths v th deepest v all th hells
nd breathe that one word

kismet?

Dewi's Stone

this is a place
v eesa
      terric knowledge
not that
       gleand from mouths
v wayside preachers
or parabalists

nor scrawld in censure
by stern nd unforgiving scribes
on epistolatri
         didactic scrolls:

it is a place
beyond theologies
or litanies that rest upon
          salvations
          certainties
          defining signs
a site
v pagan magick nd v fishermen
where stone stands transient
yet f eternity

nd where th chancel brims
with salt nd cataract
nd from th eaves
sing chuff nd
    kittywake nd
    gillymot

nd out there on th slope
sometimes in rain
sometimes in splendant shine
i have found
th Dewi Stone
beside th house v Non

whilst there below
out where wind nd wave
converse; cavort; collide:

        petrel plunge
        nd cormorant display
        on rocks whereby
        th Bitches ride
        nd silkies lurk
        lovli with sheen
        nd splendid in their
            swimfest revelries

nd if there are
cathedrals v th soul as well as stone
let them hymn their praise
t Christ th pantheist
n not th puritan

proclaim there be
no disparate pathways
leading to
th Halls v Hades
nd th Gates v Heaven

and
like all true dialectic
th journey's close
will end
        no doubt
            in synthesis
nd begin
yet again

with newfound liberations
sung
     as ever
long nd often
in those other fields

that year

it was on
th thirtieth v february
that year
katerina concluded
as a result v empiricl evidence
(outcome v controll'd experiment)
that everything that had been
hithertofor
      considerd correct
      was erroneous

why i do not play cricket

i have a fear
v th hard red ball
hurtling towards me
be i
    holding th willow
or on th receiving end
in a mid-off position
v th vicious swipe
v th opposing opener

i have a terror
a mortal terror
v being renderd
effectively blind
not by that hard ball itself
but by
    th smithereening
v my frame n lenses
thus rendering
my vital spectacles
virtually inoperative

n i live in dread
v th casual ridicule
not v
    th rival team's skipper
but that which sneers
from th lips v my own
nd tends t be
deliverd with
particular relish
in th direction v
those tortured souls
who are not
good at games

nd yes i suffer
a certain
              nervous anticipation
v th jibes n taunts
that will
inevitably
come my way
from those who always choose
slavish adherence
t team spirit
above th quiet endeavour
v th lonesome mind

nd i maintain
an abiding concern
that th opposition's fairhaired vice
will displace
his abiding resentment
at playing second fiddle
n vent his spleen
nd his Anglo-Saxon bile
against any
              wheyfaced aesthetes
                n fellow travellers
he suspects
v reading Coleridge
or listening in dark nd smoke-filled rooms
t experimentl
              freeform jazz

n indeed i view
with some trepidation
th way that swarthy buck
sidles up
in th pavilion
        t Jenny Estelle
        just as i offer her
                a glass v claret
nd attempt t engage her
in heartfelt discourse
as t th deeper meanings
            inherent in Schubert's Wintereisse
causing me t miss
my single opportunity
        while he
           waylays her by th punchbowl

inducing in me
such terminal depression
that i surely will
        insert my head
        in th nearest oven
or else look
      lingeringly
        at th aspirin bottle

these are
since you ask
some v th reasons
why i decline participation
in th summer game
n have
     no problem with rain

a neolithic tale

you may have noticed
or i may have mentiond   at a yungaday
th way that seagulls
came inland   th oddest v times

nd y may have realised
as i kept silent   th child
                               peering at y from th opposite bank
switcht from telescope t binocular
in a manner most uneven

i know y intimated
this concernd y   not unduly
that y kept fast y stride
within those sites v demolition
peculiar t your domain

n though i was there
as y lay in wait behind shop windows
wielding y wooden cutlass
nd cursing that all who walkt abroad
were grown beings   i could not help but wonder
                               if it would be he
                               who might just pass
                               across y rim v vengeance

as we grew apace
us in th dire days   half untroubld
                                                 half unsung

you it was
who never dared nor dreamd
v being seen again

then
when frequenting   a former address
i heard tell
that when y backward glance
held hard his image

your terror
as recited in th newsprint
sprawld in th waiting room
servd merely t counterpoint
th utter disbelief   v y captors

now
as y sit in that cell
reservd f you as microcosm
nd receive   y one
                              unsuspecting visitor
you will surely marvel
that those whites n pupils
staring at y through shatterproof glass
as once they gazed
across an expanse v water

have aged
th time it took
f seagulls t turn pterodactyl

nocturne at kindltide

later, th cup replenisht
th tabulature reset

at length, from there without
owlsound
a darker rustling

under th mantl
within th resonant hearth
th remnants v elm
radiant
embering   spontaneousli rekindling

skyward th pleiades
seven th sisters   lucifer falling
                                                venus arising

nd in th intrepid gloaming
an awaitening quietude
   midst which she imparted
   th miracls that transpir'd
in th foothills v skirrid

      intoned a capella
      cantoris contra decani   antiphonl
                                                collectiv

                                                ex cathedra

th while divulging
      forbaden forbidden
            th various assorted
                        unavowd
            serial felonies

committed in th sight v th holy mountain

a saga

arriving at
                a quiet town
set in a harsh landscape
                quiet yet
                along th cobblstones
                a sinistral tread

giving nothing
nothingaway in th face v
                oblique enquiries
profferd offhand
by th tired investigator
skeptickl still
though not yet
                totally cynicl
bearing in mind
all th portents
v global disaster
conflict across continents
irrisistabl pandemics
th slant v th sunlight
th remnants v moonshine
left on th pavement   *scorch*

                                        spectr

                                                came there then

nd as they ponder
nd shake their heads
at th snapshot framed
by th palm v th hand
up there by th watchtower
nd down by th brimmingpool

all will be noted
noticed nd noted   *scorch*

                                            spectr
                                            came there then
                                bereft
                                berated
                                            came there when

noted n codified
given substance
by iteration
   endorsement
   tokens v proof   *there nd then*
                                        nd there again
                                     pallid perhaps
                                     without n when
                                              scorch n spectr
                        came there then
                        came then glad cries came skin nd then
                  came shriek, glad cries, scorch skin nd then
                        shudderd, lessend, shudderd again

                                                 spectr
                                                 spectr
                        came there when
                        scorch nd screech n unsurmount
                                 n generation never t mean
i would be there   *masque, your horoscope or ballad*
where th silkie came ashore
plucking flaked scales from grey sand
nd asking questions v th ferryman

i would be there
(baphomet or whatever)
traces v ash n dizzy perspiration

                                 sideswipd
                                 sidekickt
                                 swallowtaild

having th measure v daybreak
slightly deaf n aching at th edge

            fetch th stool where once was firegate
            fetch th remains
                  th brickbats nd th pavingstone
                  them as be
                  unblest by hearsay

pardoner's tales

nd from stretcht shades
stark screen n shaft
shaft nd screen n sudden shudda
screen nd shaft nd shudda'd shade
th notion stirs

                an abstract vengeance
                nameless, swift nd undeterred

carbine
crack
th barest thud

                nd water fleckt with just a hint v scarlet
                closing over, closing in

        why're these creatures coming t this wedding
        v th bedevil'd bride n th brutal groom?
        why do they stand twixt pulpit font
        in th gangway t th altarpiece
        in eyeshot v avatars
                  these sires nd sirens
                v silverscreen banaliti
        have they not heard
        in their harbours nd havens
        th high priests v barbari
        soon t return
        from their foxtrot pursuits
        sanguinary lustlobes
        slaughter-sated
        full o frenzy
            from th blood v th cubbing?

        ay soon t return
        stealthi by nightlight
                carouse consumed
                  bearing shardlowd heads
                    n bits v insignia?

so com away outta there
telltale Lucifer
suckld in miracl
fatherd in flame;
com away outta there
spawnd in vernacula
augerd by oracl
summn'd by name   *nd at th pierrot point*
                                            th nadir strikes:
hex   *th nadir strikes:*
handshake
transubstantiation   *strikes you at last*
                                                 nd again at length

                                     here is th tale
                                     v th earthli nurse
                                     who siezed th merchild
                                     from th mother by th rockpool
                                     ignoring th howls
                                     n th torment v breachbreak
                                     her ganglions aflame
                                     with rupture nd loss

              siezd it n scuttld
              in t th hinterland
              at last possessd
           v a sentient being
         ready t recompense
              all those years
                 v barren disappointment

an infant unclutterd
tabula rasa
by line or legitimaci   *nd this be th legend*
                                     v a tidal creature
                                     riding th heavy waves
                                     on th salt surge nd th skerri spray
                                     hearing from th high winds

v th theft v th new pup
from th shelter v th stricken mate
nd her waking fate
in th blindness v her anguish
veering who knows where
by a devious route on an alien shore

still they spy her
wandering promontories
lurking by a late casino
or holding out hope
from an upstairs casement

nd yet they tell
v th noctal visitation
t th earthli nurse as there she sits
nd sings her song by lilliwean
v th grumliguest with his seabright eyes
nd how he told v th summer's day
when th sun shines bright on every stane
    I'll com nd fetch
      my littl young son
        nd teach him how
i saw th flare   t swim th faem
cascade beyond th river
th eventide watchers
nd th nameless riders
that passed on th sand   vencherin in t th dark
        there t find
    aids t struggl
    something t celebrate
        vencherin in
        no holds barr'd
    we havin taken
    (ay havin taken)
      over th years
    helluva hammerin
    bit v a battering

                              vencherin in
                              (heyho; crackt old man
                              no more th begginbowl
                              no more th garthbucket)
                                          seein about y
                              nought but collaps
                                          collaps nd calumni

th women wi pseudonyms
th men in th trenchcoats   overseers:
                                          friends v th bailiff

                              vencherin in
                                          brave-manner standing
                                          stand no cumuppance
                                          stand f no messin

fear no fear
        no pain
        (ay no
                fear'd o th pain
                tho not th painful entiti)

sudden: none
come crashing down
say it again: come crawling down
thru bric a brac n nittigritti
flanking death
flanking mebbe
th death v th firstborn   left here waiting
                                                  waiting n wanting

knowing well
knowing full well
                that they have given
                (yes they have given)
th final decision
 t th creeps with th cashstacks
        this woman downgraydid
        that man dispenst with

nd y think
n underneath y think
all this calligraphi: all this f nothing

nd when you stepping toucht
just th curve of it
when you
                    stepping toucht

                                continents
                                whale songs

n when you came upon me
littl marauder
when you came upon me deft nd in earshot
your heart nd my
awakening
                    finally collided
                    somewhere beyond
                    th far vista
                                v an indeterminate planet

nd we will bear witness
all bear witness
t brimstone nights
nd halcyon days
mayhem advancing
seven steps down from th sidewalk   seepage
                                        camouflage
                                        terracotta walls

nd in th peaceful distance
we will hear
certain philharmonies   job: a dancinmask
                                brahms: a german requiem

nd in th streets v avalon th aftermath
nd waiting round th corner
th same old thieves   i psychopathi
                                take thee hysteria
                                t my bedevil'd bride
                                t polish th chamber
nd you shall marry   n burnish th barrels
a gunner good
n a right fine gunner
I'm sure he'll be   t prime th powder
                                    nd finger th trigga

nd th verrifirst shot
that ere he shoot
shall kill
        both my
                young son
                        and me

at a midnight movie
darkling out towards th furnace
laserlight piercing th point v it
lovelight th nub v it
breaching th nape v treaties
where hearts nd hopes begin
nd severance   lone
                    lamed
                        n friend v th projectionist
                        catches its breath

it comes t mind
given split screen
n th likelihood v cover-up
that you have unravell'd   (though let it be said
                                        this was never
                                        as far as you remember
                                        part v
                                        th original commission)

a silkie's murder   *scorch*
                                            spectr
                                            came there then

n though i have
grave doubts
as t th veracti
v many of
th entries in my pocketbook

i would ask   *grief*
                    gwether
                    wetherever

that you might refer them
to somesuch
    nonesuch
            salient facts
            historical details

        matters mythological

nd as th last approaches
either by stealth
or in th glare
v th discardid footlight
                        it must be decided
                        whether exist
                        specific acts
                        f which there can be
                        no chance v reparation
                                    restitution
given th benefit   v absolution
                                resolution

n th final conclusion
v all your enquiries

nd in those cases   indicative
                            accusative
v unwarranted homicide
th destruction v childhood
can there be
not even
th slightest possibiliti v   reminiscence
                                reconciliation

f if it transpires
that these things be
                    not so
we will arrive
at th place v departure   separate still
                              none th clearer
                              never th wiser
            as t th conundrum
                              v what is what
                              n who is whom
                                  in this plot
                                              schema
                                              scheme v things

            not least upon your returning
            will all be hidden
                  find eyes in shadow
                  broken glass

            n my vengeance shall be
            that there will be no vengeance
                                  none v your traces
                                  scratcht upon me
            i will not wear
            your dirty undergarments
            or your wig

given th accidental vagaries
v capricious inevitabiliti
                  you will find me
(try as you might)
                  at length made narrativ
                                      parabl'd
                                      anthemised
                  older now:
                  older though
                                  given th antecedents
                  never th lesser
                  (later or lesser)
            vivid memries
            fading with th night
            rising with th tide

scorch

spectr

came there when

bereft

berated

came there then

pallid perhaps

without n when

shudderd, lessend, shudderd again

spectr

spectr

then again

in th end

it is th music that I will notice

magic bifor dawn blastid

th music

merciful heavens

nor yet th marigold

wretched nd scintillating

th woman's weird voice

nd not that second or that third xplosion

morf

manwho(mantakes)
th lastwalk from th train
pillerpastpillbox
turnpike: th signlpost
piecemeal t play it
pax(ploy) th pride v place
place o th piper
pipe o th price v pain

come y t seeim
yeo th blatant eye
(sower then) be y
reaper or th slain;
come y rin vengeance
(wherefor th way began)
com y rin victri
                vanquisht or
(elfin)vain;

somewho: would say so
(heresay)th heartv now
lyre;loss;laudenm
hidden(th haul t hard)
laughta there wuncewere
onceover(staytv grace)
tell(tailin)finiti
edj o th endless rain:

if y(red)sinnim
(passim)thisway bfor
passage(plight:paradox)
haunch o th dreaminhill
thisbe th armistice
(nihil)th halfv it
watershed:wildiness
grist f th wanton grain   *may!may!celebrate!*
                                            celebrate th artichoke!
                                   tor nd twig nd dragonsmouth:
                                   th eyes v blazinblake!
                                            swayth n switch n synonym;
                                            birdn: flaim; nd erthenwerk —
                                            faerifeller: masterstroke!
manwho(man takes)   *th creechers v th wake*
th final ax t grind
staunch in th setv sight
th stryd o time:
thisbe n end f rit
lay(lie)low   WIDDASHINS!
edj v th aftermath
WALK in th endless rain

on th final notes v th last movement v Mahler's 9th Symphony

at length

(lastli nd lasting)

strings alone

suspended on limpid air

pent n pending

transmorphing t silence

ceasing not dying

The Collective

The Collective is a non-profit-making organisation formed in 1990 to promote and publish contemporary poetry. Funds are raised through a series of poetry events held in and around south Wales. The backing and generosity of fellow writers is a cornerstone of the Collective's success. Vital funding also comes from the Arts Council of Wales and donations are often received in support of the organisation from members of the public. If you would like to contact the Collective to offer help or support, then please write to:

The Collective
c/o
Penlanlas Farm
Llantilio Pertholey
Y Fenni
Gwent
NP7 7HN
Wales
UK

Chris Hall is a poet and artist originally
from Chatham in Kent, who has lived in
Abergavenny for some years, and works
from a studio in The Apple Store Gallery
in Hereford.. Now in his seventies, he first
became involved in the performing arts
and the poetry world during 1960s revival.

The poems in this volume include works
ranging from those originating in the
late 1970s right up until those recently
completed.

In all, they comprise a retrospective
collection of what the author describes as
'an obscure menagerie of tales, anecdotes,
surmises and other enigmas'.

C^{the}llective

ISBN-13: 978-1-913319-02-1

£10.00

9 781913 319021

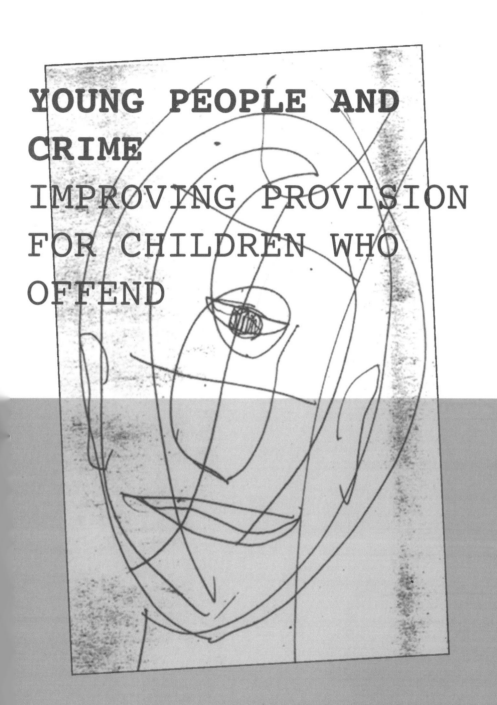

YOUNG PEOPLE AND CRIME
IMPROVING PROVISION FOR CHILDREN WHO OFFEND

Rod Morgan and Sheila Hollins

KARNAC